CONTENTS

INTRODUCTION

Frogs are a joy to keep. They can be housed in an outdoor enclosure specially built for the purpose, or in tanks inside the house. In summary, frogs:

1. Don't bark or bite.
2. Don't need expensive food.
3. Adapt readily to captivity.
4. Need only a small amount of space.
5. Never demand 'walkies' or to be entertained.
6. Don't make awful smells.
7. Can be left alone while you take brief holidays.
8. Are very easy to keep.
9. Rarely need veterinary care.
10. Are endlessly fascinating to watch.

Of all the immensely varied animals that have come and gone throughout our family's life, frogs would be top of the popularity stakes.

Besides these appealing features, frogs are endearing little creatures, which deserve to be better understood. We humans can learn a great deal about our environment through the keeping of various species of frogs, and in Australia, there are so many species that one may keep, that the difficulty is which species to choose. The even more difficult choice is where to stop. Having once kept a few frogs, the hobby may well become an addiction, and assume epic proportions. At this point, frog tanks will appear in every room, and the evening chorus will be a fascinating blend of the calls of frogs of all kinds, filling the air with their musical voices.

Sadly, some enthusiastic first time frog keepers become rapidly disillusioned as their frogs inexplicably die, and the keepers are left wondering what went wrong. This brings us to the need for a simple, user friendly book to explain the basic requirements of frog keeping for the novice or beginner frog keeper. However, there is no substitute for spending time with an experienced keeper.

LICENSING

In Australia, it is illegal to remove frogs from the wild, and a licence is needed to keep many of our native frog species. As licence requirements differ in individual states, you will need to contact your own state's Department of Natural Resources/Conservation/Environment as the case may be. Usually obtaining a licence is simply a matter of filling in the appropriate forms and paying the required fee, which depends on the species you wish to keep. The same licence requirements apply to the sale and purchase of frogs. Only those with the appropriate state licence may sell frogs, so when you obtain your licence, you may only purchase your frogs from a licensed person; to do otherwise is a serious offence.

FROG BIOLOGY

Frogs are amphibians, which have been around for probably more than 180 million years. Like other amphibians they are vertebrates, i.e. they have backbones. They are also ectothermic, meaning that they rely on external sources for their body heat. Some people use the term 'cold blooded', but as this term has taken on other meanings over time, usually describing cruelty or inability to feel pain, it's best to stick to ectothermic to describe frogs.

Frogs have soft skins, which are highly permeable, taking moisture in, and also absorbing anything else that may be in the air or water. This is probably one reason for the dramatic decline in frog species world-wide. Frogs' absorbent skins will also absorb any pollutants or toxins that are present in their environment.

Most frog species require water to breed. Eggs are laid by the female and then fertilised externally by the male. The eggs hatch into tadpoles, which have gills, and spend all of their time in the water. Tadpoles eat non stop until they develop limbs and emerge from the water as air breathing animals. Gradually these little frogs, usually called morphlings, absorb their tails, a built in source of nutrients, and then set about growing by eating insects. The entire process of change from tadpole to frog is termed metamorphosis, the same term as is used for the changes from egg to larva to pupa to adult insect. Fully developed frogs have no tails, and are scientifically classed as anurans, or tailless amphibians.

Basic Rules

Before going into the specific details of housing, it is well worth emphasising the few absolute rules of keeping frogs. They **must** have ...

1. Clean water, free from chemicals of any kind. This may mean collecting rain water or treating the water from the tap to remove chemicals such as chlorine.

2. Clean air with no pollutants. This is critical and will mean no fumes such as gas, cigarette smoke, incense smoke, or aerosol sprays of any kind in the house.

3. Both land and water areas, the size of each depending on the species being kept (See individual species information, page 22-36).

4. Live insects of an appropriate size, as food. Despite what you may have heard, mice and raw meat are not suitable food for frogs, as frogs are totally insectivorous. Mice and pieces of meat have far too much protein content, and can cause kidney damage and the death of your frogs.

5. Full spectrum UV light, either daylight or special reptile lights available from pet shops. The light must not have to shine through glass or plastic, as these prevent penetration of the UV rays to the frogs.

So no matter whether your enclosure is indoors or outside, these rules must be followed if your frog keeping is to be the delight that it should be for both you and the frogs. Mastering these few simple rules is the basis of good frog husbandry.

OUTDOOR ENCLOSURES

An outdoor enclosure is entirely appropriate, as long as the frogs you intend to keep are local to your area, or come from an area with a very similar climate to your own. Clearly, keeping tropical frogs out of doors in the far south, or keeping cold climate frogs outdoors in the tropics simply will not work. So outdoor enclosures can only be used with the above provisos.

Having established that your climate suits the frogs you want to keep, an outdoor enclosure can be as simple or as elaborate as you like. Keep in mind the basic rules, and the natural environment in which such frogs would normally live, ie. desert, forest, trees, swamps, etc. Site the enclosure where it gets both sun and shade; preferably the sun should not directly strike the pond itself, thus keeping the water less prone to algae build up. You can achieve this shade with shade cloth or better still with solid roofing material over part of the enclosure. However, tadpoles will feed happily on algae, so it's not a major drama unless the water actually becomes slimy. For tree frogs, some tall plants suitable to your local area may be used, and the frogs will climb into these to hide, stalk their prey, or bask in the sun when the urge strikes them. Tall grasses are good, as are soft leafed ferns.

The floor of the enclosure should be planted, and thick planting is much better from the frogs' point of view. Outdoor enclosures are usually made from untreated wood and wire mesh, with a partial solid roof. This allows sufficient light to penetrate without the filtering effect of glass or plastic. It will also allow free ventilation and prevent humidity and heat build up which would occur if using glass. On the face of it, plastic mesh may be an appealing alternative to wire from the point of view of price. However, any self respecting rat, mouse, dog, cat or fox will make short work of gaining entry through plastic mesh, and will be inside the enclosure creating chaos faster than you would believe possible. This applies not only to the walls of enclosures, but also to the roof. Non climbing frogs should have a smooth material on the inside, up to 100mm from the ground level as they sometimes damage their noses on wire.

It is imperative too, that there should be no small holes through which frogs may escape. It is the solemn duty of all frogs to escape from their housing, and if it is at all possible, they will do so in the shortest possible time. Making your enclosure absolutely escape proof right from the start will save lots of anguish further down the track. Ensure that the wire mesh is of a suitable size so that very small frogs cannot escape, and that the insects you feed to the frogs remain inside the enclosure. If there is a chance of predators of any kind, then the mesh should extend well below ground level to prevent predators digging into the enclosure, or burrowing frogs digging out.

Outdoor enclosures should contain plenty of hiding places, and these can be plants, branches, stones, leaf litter or pieces of bark, and there must be access to water at all times. A pond set into the ground is ideal, but a large dish of water is just as acceptable to the frogs. Whichever way you choose to provide water, make sure that the frogs can get in and out easily. It seems impossible, but be assured that frogs can drown if they are unable to leave the water. So provide plenty of easy entry and exit points by having plants either growing in the pond or trailing into it from the edges. Sloping sides rather than vertical ones make entry and exit a great deal easier for the frogs. The actual depth of the water can vary hugely according to your preferences (and inclination to dig!), but should not be less than 300mm (check for local council rulings on depth of water allowed!), and **must** be partially shaded to avoid over heating.

There are many suitable plants for use in frog ponds, and your local nursery should be able to advise you on varieties for the job. Broadly speaking, most plants suitable for outdoor goldfish ponds are suitable also for frogs. Try to stick with native plant species if possible, as some exotics can run amok and choke the pond. Bog plants can be used around the edges of the pond, and these will provide good places for the frogs to rest. Again, consult your local nursery for advice on plants suitable to your area. Plants in pots are also appropriate, and can be moved around for visual effect or planted out when the effect seems satisfactory. Avoid potting mixes though, as these often contain artificial fertilisers, and insecticides, which can be toxic, not just to insects, but also to

Above ground enclosure photo by Mark Davidson.

wash plants to remove any traces of horticultural spray residue. Don't make the mistake of trying to keep goldfish in the same pond as the frogs use. The fish will eat the frogs' eggs and small tadpoles. If you want to reduce mosquitoes breeding in the frog pond, then beg, borrow or buy some Murray River Rainbowfish. Hopefully these will keep any mosquito problem to a minimum. NB. Native plants around the pond will attract native insects for the frogs.

If you select an 'in ground pond', then you will need to provide a way of cleaning it periodically, both to keep mosquitoes down and to remove the build up of algae that will grow in the water, more so if the pond itself is in the sun. A suitable pump with a filter will keep the water moving and keep the water cleaner. However, most frogs prefer to spawn in still water, so the pump should create only gentle movement that allows some corners of the pond to remain relatively still. When the frogs do spawn, the pump will need to be turned off to avoid filtering the eggs and small tadpoles out of the water. It is preferable to remove the small tadpoles with a fine mesh net once they have hatched from the eggs, and rear them on in a tank until they morph. They can be put back into the enclosure when they have reached a similar size to the established occupants.

Of course a removable bowl makes the job of cleaning a great deal simpler, even if it may not look as natural as an 'in ground' pond. You can always 'naturalise' it with a few flat rocks and plants around the edge. Another advantage of a removable bowl is that after spawning, you can simply remove the bowl and the spawn for raising the tadpoles, and replace the bowl with another suitable one. There are many variations on the outdoor enclosure. Some people build them on heavy duty castors, so that the whole enclosure can be moved if required. Another possibility is to build the enclosure on a stand, using the frame of a glass tank, but replacing the glass with fine mesh. A hinged wire mesh lid on a frame can be provided and that will allow easy access for cleaning, feeding and general maintenance. Make sure that you allow for drainage taps as for indoor enclosures.

Existing aviaries can be altered to provide good frog housing, usually by replacing the aviary mesh with finer mesh and adding a pond and suitable planting. If the existing structure has a roof that is zinc coated, this will need to be replaced, as the water run off may contain small amounts of zinc, which is toxic to frogs. If you are using an existing aviary or any walk in frog enclosure, be aware that frogs will hide under rocks and ground litter, so you will need to ensure a clear path for your own entry and walking space. In outdoor enclosures, ensure that no pollutants by way of herbicides, pesticides or artificial fertilisers are used anywhere near the site of the enclosure. Of course you could always let your imagination run riot and provide scenic rock pools and the like, but I doubt your frogs would be any happier than with a simple construction that allows for the basics of clean water, clean air, suitable light and suitable food.

INDOOR ENCLOSURES

Indoor enclosures are the most popular housing for frogs, and they add the benefit of being able to see and hear your frogs at all times. This also often means that the frogs will be afforded more attention in the way of feeding, water changes and general maintenance. Because the enclosures are always in view, you are therefore more likely to notice anything that may go wrong or need your immediate attention. As with outdoor housing, the indoor enclosure can be as simple or elaborate as you like, or as finances permit. But a simple enclosure is every bit as satisfactory as an elaborate one from the frogs' point of view, as long as the basic requirements are met. A glass tank is the most obvious choice for a start, as glass is easy to keep clean just by wiping with clean water and paper towelling, and you will always have a clear view of your frogs. The size of the tank will depend on the number of frogs you intend to keep. A word of warning here though; once you have sampled the joys of frog keeping, you will very likely become totally addicted, and the tank will never be big enough, nor will you ever have enough tanks to house all the different species of frogs that you want to keep. As an absolute minimum, a 600mm long tank will do for several very small frogs, but a 1200mm tank allows for landscaping and a much happier environment for the inhabitants. Crowded frogs become stressed frogs, and stressed frogs die. So avoid very small tanks, as these are sure to frustrate you after a short time, and you will undoubtedly wish that you had purchased a bigger one in the first place.

Whether the tank is horizontal or vertical is determined by whether you want to keep tree frogs, in which case a vertical tank is appropriate, or terrestrial frogs, in which case the horizontal tank will be more satisfactory. Likewise, the amount of land or water area is determined by the species you want to keep, so make these species decisions before buying the tank to save yourself trying to adapt something that isn't really up to the job. It's best not to mix different species in one tank. It is possible to buy tanks with a glass divider between water and land areas, and such tanks are by far the better buy. They should also be provided with drainage holes and taps, preferably in both sections, so that water can be changed easily by just turning on the taps. Siphoning, or scooping the water out with dippers is tiresome, and you will need to flush the land area through occasionally, as it becomes fouled with frog droppings and dead insects. With a dual tap system built into the tank, you will be able to water the plants in the enclosure without the substrate becoming waterlogged and fouled by standing water. For most frogs, about a quarter to a third of the tank could be water and the rest land area, since most frogs spend little time in the water.

Tank Lid

The tank will need a close fitting lid. Make no mistake about the fact that frogs have an endless urge to escape, and will do so sneakily and under cover of darkness. When purchasing a tank, a lid is usually supplied. Make sure that it fits very firmly so that not even the most determined frog could find a way out. The lid is best made from fly screen mesh on a wooden or metal frame. Glass can form part of the lid, but the UV rays from the light you install cannot pass though glass, so wire mesh is a better option and permits the free flow of air, preventing humidity build up. For tropical frogs, perhaps half the lid could be glass to retain some humidity. Make sure that the mesh size is appropriate to contain the size of insects you will be feeding to the frogs. Plastic mesh is quite suitable, but bear in mind that it can sag, if anything (like the family cat!) likes to sit on top of the tank and watch the frogs. It is really very helpful from the point of view of ease of maintenance if the lid is in two parts, or hinged in the middle, so that you don't have to remove the whole lid when feeding or cleaning any part of the tank. Holding a one piece lid while trying to drop live insects in and keep the frogs from escaping, while also balancing a fluorescent light is a hazardous exercise. Hinge the lid or have it made in two pieces for safety's sake.

Lighting

Correct lighting for frogs is not an optional extra. It is vital for the health of the frogs. Lighting must be of the correct type; a specifically made fluorescent reptile light purchased from a pet shop, and one that emits both UVA and UVB rays is the only satisfactory type. These are called full spectrum lights, and will need to be replaced about every one to two years, or as recommended by the manufacturer (the old fluorescent light from the shed simply will not do!). UVA light promotes natural behaviour and UVB light is essential to synthesise Vitamin D3, which is needed in the absorption of calcium, so an absence of this light will cause bone deformities and a failure to grow. Fix the fluorescent tube about 300 to 400mm. above the substrate on the floor of the tank. Any further away than this and the rays simply cannot reach far enough to have the required effect. Tree frogs of course will sit up on branches close to the light source. In general terms, most frogs are active at night, but the need for UV light still exists, as many frogs like to bask under the light. The light can be switched on in the morning and off after sunset, tying this in with the variations in day length throughout the seasons. You could use an electric timer for this if you prefer. Don't compromise. Purchase the correct light in the beginning and you'll know that you've done the right thing by your frogs.

Photo by Darren Green.

Substrate & Furnishings

Substrate is the material placed on the bottom of the land area of the tank. It needs to be free draining so that the area can be washed through periodically to prevent a build up of bacteria, and the frogs' droppings. It also needs to be non-toxic and completely inert, ie. it has little or no chemical reaction. Coarse aquarium gravel is the most suitable for the bottom layer, because it is easy to wash through with water and drains well. The down side is that frogs may inadvertently swallow small pieces of the gravel and these can block the intestines and kill the frog. So the gravel needs to be contained right at the bottom, and covered with a softer material like palm peat. Place a piece of wire mesh over the drainage hole so that loose gravel doesn't clog the tap.

You will need to wash the land area through on a regular basis to keep it clean, and the more frogs there are in the tank, the more often this needs to be done. Also, smaller areas need to be washed through more often than large ones, and more washes are needed in summer than in winter. With a small area, wash the substrate through about once a week to ensure that the tank doesn't become too acidic for the frogs.

A good way to set up the tank is to cover the several centimetres of gravel with wire or plastic mesh, which is tucked firmly down around the gravel along the edges of the land area. Then the mesh can be covered with a few more centimetres of coconut shell fibre (often sold as palm peat or coco peat), and available in brick form at hardware stores, some supermarkets and garden centres. It is a simple matter to soak the brick in water and then crumble the peat like material so that it is reasonably level over the mesh. Palm peat is relatively inert, and contains no toxins to harm the frogs.

Because the fibres are small and soft, if the frogs ingest any, it cannot harm them. You will find that after placing the palm peat, it will compact down nicely and form a soft floor for the enclosure. Ordinary garden peat is not suitable, because its pH is a little too acidic for frogs. The palm peat can also be allowed to dry out, or be kept moist with the use of a small hand held mist sprayer, depending on the environment that a particular species of frog prefers.

Then you can furnish the enclosure, keeping in mind the environment that your frogs would naturally inhabit. Some smooth or flat rocks are good for frogs to sit on and sleep or lurk, and as the frogs will use these, their bodies will remain relatively free of palm peat crumbs. If you have tree frogs, they will need branches to climb. The branches should be perfectly clean and dry, and free from any substances or insects that may cause harm. Dead branches are preferred, as they contain no potentially hazardous sap. Always soak selected branches in hot water for a day or two, then dry them out on a low heat in the oven to ensure that everything is as clean and germ free as possible. It's a good idea to also clean the gravel by washing it in clean water several times before putting it in the tank. Even gravel purchased from aquarium shops will need cleaning first to remove dust and bacteria. Clean and bake the rocks too, and be sure that there are no sharp corners or edges that pose potential harm to the frogs' soft skins.

Plants can be included in the furnishings of course, with their roots anchored in the gravel and palm peat. Some suitable plants for indoor tanks are Mondo grass, native violet (*Viola hederacea*), Peace Lilies *(Spathyphllum)*, the Fruit Salad Plant (*Monstera deliciosa*) the Happy Plant (*Dracaena marginata*) and many other indoor species that like a well lit, moist environment. **Always** remove all of the potting mix or soil from living plants and wash them thoroughly in clean water before planting in the tank to avoid introducing artificial fertilisers or 'foreign' bacteria.

There is of course no reason that your planting could not be wholly made up of plastic plants, some of which look remarkably real and extremely attractive in a tank. Do be certain though to wash plastic plants thoroughly too before use. Plastic has the benefit of being easily removed and cleaned when the need arises. I prefer living plants though, even though they grow and can get untidy, and large frogs will probably trample them underfoot. I suspect that the frogs like them too.

Water Quality

The quality of the water supplied to frogs is of major importance. In many areas, ordinary tap water is suitable, with a few provisos. Firstly, your local water authority will be able to tell you the average pH of the water it supplies. The pH scale indicates acidity or alkalinity of the water, and to be suitable for frogs, the reading needs to be close to 7.0, which indicates neutral. A figure much higher or lower than this will mean that the water is either too alkaline or too acidic for frogs, and may need adjusting with a suitable product from aquarium shops. Having said this however, I have always found Australian town water to be of a quality to be used for frogs without any chemical additives.

The second proviso is that most town water is treated with chlorine and possibly other chemicals. Chlorinated water is very bad for frogs, but fortunately it is a simple matter to de-chlorinate. Just leave the water in a clean plastic bucket out in the sun for a day or two, and the chlorine will dissipate, leaving you with clean water. Keep this bucket clearly marked 'Frogs Only' and don't let it be used for any other purpose like car washing. Chlorine neutralisers can be purchased from aquarium shops, but I always prefer just to leave the water to de-chlorinate itself in a day or two. Tank water is usually O.K., but you need to know that on its way to the tap it hasn't been fouled with bird droppings, a build up of dead leaves, pine needles, zinc roof coating, or any other 'foreign' materials. Test kits are available from aquarium shops so that you can test the pH and hardness/softness of tank water, and you need to be very careful about what the water has passed through or over on its way to the tap.

Rainwater is great, and can always be used for frogs. Collect it in a non-metal container though. And speaking of metal, copper pipes in water systems can contaminate the water that passes through, so take care of this hazard too. Frequently only the hot water has copper piping, but it's worth checking just the same. If using hot water to wash any frog furnishings, always rinse with cold water before placing them back into the tank.

You can add plants to the water section of the tank, using suitable species obtained from aquarium shops. It helps the frogs if plants can trail down over the divider into the water. Bearing in mind that frogs can drown, you will need to make sure that their access to and from the water is made easy by way of large rocks placed in the water. Not all frogs are able to climb, so be aware of this and put rocks in several places in the water area to prevent the frogs drowning. Importantly, place rocks in all the corners, the place where frogs are especially likely to drown. Rocks must be completely stable to avoid trapping frogs.

Water changes must be made frequently to maintain cleanliness. The more frogs, the more often the water will need to be changed, and the smaller the volume of water, the more changes are needed. As a very basic guide, change water weekly in small tanks to avoid the water becoming fouled due to droppings and dead insects. Large droppings or insects can be fished out with a net on a daily basis. Don't ever clean the inside of the tank, either land or water areas, with anything except plain, clean water and paper towels when frogs are in residence.

Humidity Requirements

Some frogs like a humid environment and others prefer their enclosure to be quite dry on the land area. Generally speaking, match the humidity level to that which occurs in the frogs' native habitat. Don't make the mistake of assuming that all frogs like to be wet all of the time. The reality is that most of them don't even enter the water except to absorb water through the skin, or until it's their spawning time, and excess humidity can cause bacteria to build up, and this may be detrimental to the frogs' health. Always provide dry areas in the frog tank. The highly decorative waterfalls, fountains and mist makers that look so appealing in displays, are **not** necessary, and may even harm the frogs, keeping the whole tank environment wet and humid all the time.

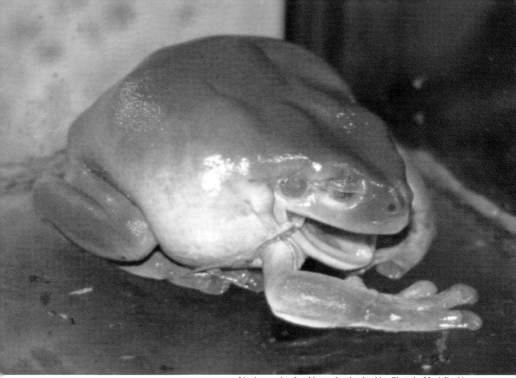
Litoria caerulea sloughing and eating its skin. Photo by Mark Davidson.

Heating

This will be necessary if you are keeping frogs that come from a much warmer climate than your local one, even if you are keeping the frogs indoors. Heating if needed for particular species, is noted in the *Species* section. The most suitable type of heating for frogs is an aquarium heater placed in the water. Aquarium heaters are inexpensive, long lasting, and having once been set to the correct temperature, rarely need adjusting. Remember though that because of the heating, there will be more evaporation, so you will need to keep the water topped up to avoid burning the heater out if the water level drops too low; the correct level will be marked on the heater when you buy it.

Set the tank up, then place the heater in the water, and spend a day or two letting the heat stabilise at the temperature you want before adding the frogs, or you face the risk of cooking the frogs if fluctuations occur. It is of course necessary to have a thermometer in the tank to check the water temperature as you are setting up, and then check again periodically as a safeguard. The cheapest aquarium thermometer is quite satisfactory, and comes with a suction cap so that it will adhere to the glass inside the tank. Have the bulb of the thermometer in the water, and the temperature of the water will give you an estimate of the tank's air temperature. For example, water at 28°C will most likely give an air temperature of around 26°C or 27°C, depending on the size of the tank and the ambient temperature of the room.

Heat lamps and heat mats are dangerous when used inside an enclosure with frogs. There is a danger that the frogs will jump onto the hot surface and suffer burns, but the likelihood of electric shock is also present. DO NOT include a heat lamp in your frog furnishings. When heating the tank, close off part of the lid with glass or other solid lid in order to retain the heat. Always leave the space where the UV light shines down, clear of any obstruction. Heat mats are okay under the outside of the enclosure.

FEEDING

Frogs are insect eaters, and there's no getting away from that simple fact. So steer well away from substitute feeds, no matter how appealing they may sound, or how attractive the packaging. Frogs also prefer their insects alive and moving. Some large frogs will happily eat frozen (then thawed) insects offered to them on tweezers or forceps, and this method is useful if there is a reason to know which frog is eating or not eating, as the case may be. It's also sometimes useful if your frogs will eat pre-frozen insects, as these can then be kept when you catch or buy too many for immediate use. Crickets and 'woodies' (a commercial name for a variety of cockroach), are both suitable for freezing if you have lots at any time.

Insects of an appropriate size can be caught, or purchased from pet and aquarium shops, and with a little attention, the insects can be held until they are needed (see below). Suitable insects, depending on the size of the frogs, can be crickets, grasshoppers, houseflies, blowflies, beetles, vinegar flies (*Drosophila*); these are the little flies that lurk about compost heaps and the fruit bowl, cicadas, cockroaches, slaters, moths, wax worms, earthworms, and **occasionally,** mealworms. Having mentioned mealworms, I would only feed them to big, adult frogs, and only rarely. They would certainly be too hard for small frogs to manage. They have tough outer skins, which are hard to digest, and can cause a blockage in a frog's digestive system. The greater the variety of insects that you are able to feed, the healthier your frogs will be, and the less likely they are to become fussy 'gourmet' types that will flatly refuse any food except their particular favourite.

Many insects can be captured outside in your own garden, especially in leaf litter, under rocks or path edging, and under lights at night. A home made sweeper net can be used effectively to catch insects in long grass. Do not ever catch insects where there is a chance that you or your neighbours may have used insect baits or insecticide sprays. In this regard, it is a good idea to leave a patch of garden to go wild, where all sorts of plants and weeds will flower and attract lots of insects. This patch should be an absolute 'no go' zone for ultra tidy gardeners or for sprays or possible spray drift of any kind from nearby areas.

Frogs, like all animals, need a balanced diet for good health. So a variety of food must be offered to ensure that they obtain all the protein, fat, vitamins and minerals that they need to grow up healthy and stay that way. Be aware that most frogs have the appetites of sword swallowers, and this applies most particularly to young frogs, which need to grow quickly in the wild so that they can mature and spawn. Green Tree Frogs are the hungriest of all, but they can become over-weight as adults, so don't let them con you with that sly smile, into feeding them as adults the way they needed to eat as youngsters. Adult frogs can slow down their food requirements, especially in the season when they are not in or approaching breeding mode. (See *Species* section for breeding times of specific frogs). Insects have different nutritional values, and the following gives an approximate guide to these. But it is important to recognise that food values depend on the condition of the insects, and on the foods on which they have been reared. The main thing is to accept that variety in food is essential to keep up the supply of nutrients to your frogs.

Note: when using live food in the enclosure, also ensure that there is something for them to eat, otherwise hungry food items may be tempted to turn on the frog and cause them harm.

CRICKETS contain approximately 55% protein and 30% fat, with small amounts of calcium, phosphorus, vitamin C and fibre and contain about 52 calories per. hundred grams.

FLY LARVAE (maggots) contain almost as much calcium as crickets, but with more moisture content and more fibre than crickets, with small amounts of fat, ash, and vitamin C. 53 calories per. 100 grams. Some frogs seem to be unable to digest large, blowfly maggots, and pass them whole in their droppings; if this happens, then forget maggots in future for those frogs, or take the ghastly step of stabbing each blowfly maggot to enable the frog's digestive juices to begin to work. (Personally, I'd just forget the maggots).

WOODIES and COCKROACHES are similar, and have marginally more protein and fibre.

MEALWORMS have just over 20% protein, 15% fat, with small amounts of calcium and phosphorus and some ash, vitamin C and fibre. Restrict the feeding of these to large adult frogs, and only feed occasionally.

LOCUSTS are high in protein and low in fat, and contain high levels of phosphorus and iodine.

GRASSHOPPERS are similar to crickets.

WAXWORMS are the larvae of the pest moth of apiarists, and have over 60% protein and 21% fat, as well as vitamin C, fibre and ash. Their caloric value is a very high 182 calories per 100g. Commercially bred wax worms are very rarely available, so if obtaining these from an apiarist, take care that the worms are fat and lively, and that there are no dead, blackish worms, as these may be contaminated by a bacteria or virus, which has the potential to harm frogs.

Litoria infrafrenata eating a Bogong Moth. Photo by Leigh Johnson.

Holding Insects for Later Use

It is not possible in a book of this size to go into the complicated subject of insect breeding, but it is helpful if you know how to keep the insects you have purchased or caught, in a healthy state until you need them.

Fly Larvae (maggots) purchased from bait shops or aquarium shops, can be kept in a refrigerator in dry bran for a couple of weeks as long as the temperature doesn't fall below 4°C. To have them change into pupae and morph into flies, place into a larger container, warm them up to room temperature and wait for the hatching to begin. Make some fly sized holes in the lid of the container, and the flies will emerge to be grabbed enthusiastically by the frogs.

Mealworms can also be kept in dry bran in the refrigerator, but take care to remove the lids of containers occasionally and wipe off any condensation. Once the worms become wet, they will blacken and die.

Crickets, **woodies** and **cockroaches** should be kept above 15°C and must be fed. They can have dry food like rabbit or cat/dog pellets and will need some moist fruit or vegetable like potato, carrot, broccoli, apple or other vegetable to keep their food value up, add moisture, and to prevent them cannibalising each other.

Locusts and **grasshoppers** need a temperature over 25°C and should be fed on clean, fresh grass daily, and some dry bran.

Wax worms, if commercially produced will be packed in their own specialised diet, and need only to be kept at room temperature. Carefully remove the worms and feed as required. To allow the worms to pupate and morph into moths, empty into a larger container and keep them warm.

Remember that only healthy insects should be fed to frogs, and the insects will only be healthy if they are well fed and kept in a clean state. Old, dried out insects add nothing to a frog's diet, and in fact frogs may lose weight and eventually die of malnutrition if only presented with such food. Feed your insects well and the frogs will thrive.

Vitamin and Mineral Supplements

These are available from pet shops, and can certainly be beneficial for frogs, and calcium powder sprinkled on the insects for young, growing frogs is helpful for their growing bones. Reduce the calcium somewhat for adult frogs. Take care with these supplements, especially with vitamin D3, excess of which may cause kidney failure and arthritis. Vitamin D3 is present in the livers of whole insects, so it really isn't necessary to add a D3 powder if your frogs are getting a balanced diet and correct lighting. Just take care and use common sense with any additives, and carefully follow the directions on the packet. To add calcium/vitamin powder, place the insects in a plastic bag or container with lid, sprinkle a very small amount of the powder in, and gently shake until the insects are covered with powder before you offer them to the frogs. Powder loose in the enclosure is not an issue, just use your sprayer to remove the residue from the plants.

How often and when to feed

Most frogs are active at night, and this is when they should be fed. Insects put into the enclosure in daylight will often be missed by sleeping frogs, and will probably drown in the water. This is very frustrating. So feed when the frogs are most active, probably when you have turned the lights off, and the frogs are about their natural hunting behaviour, sneaking up and nabbing insects with great enthusiasm. Small, growing frogs should be fed daily. You'll soon get an idea of how much they need by just watching quietly. If the frogs gobble up all the insects you have offered and are still looking around, then increase their rations. If however, they seem less than enthusiastic and lots of insects end up drowning, then cut back the amount and frequency of feeding. There are no hard and fast rules here, just observation and common sense will soon tell you if you're getting it right.

BREEDING

When you have kept some frogs for a while, you will undoubtedly want to try breeding with them. Many keepers see breeding frogs as a challenge that they just have to meet, as a measure of their success as keepers. If a myriad tiny, hungry tadpoles, and masses of baby frogs sounds appealing, be warned! All those tiny mouths have to be fed, you will need more tanks, be endlessly changing water and chasing tiny escapees. Some will die and give you guilt in a major way, and there will very probably be little market for your carefully bred and fed babies anyway. But if the urge to breed frogs should strike, then you'll probably ignore the warnings and do it anyway.

Sexing

The first issue is that adult frogs are needed. Secondly, you must have both sexes. These points may be ultra obvious, but determining a frog's sex is far from obvious for a novice, and difficult even for an experienced keeper. With young frogs, there's just no way for you to determine sex, so forget it until they grow to adult size. In general, female frogs grow larger than the males. The males may have a slightly narrower abdomen, but when sitting, all adult frogs appear to have fat tummies, so that's not a lot of help.

Only the males will sing, and this is a certain way of sexing them, unless of course a female gives a short squawk as they occasionally do, and then you're messed up again. But if a frog consistently sings, then it's a male. Males in breeding condition will develop 'breeding thumbs' or nuptial pads, when the outside edges of the thumbs become thicker and darker. This is so that the male is more easily able to grasp and hold the female. Okay, so what about ensuring that you have a female? It is possible, although admittedly difficult, to see the eggs inside a female of some species through her abdomen. It's pretty tricky, and can definitely be injurious to the frog, so have a very experienced keeper show you how to do this if you really have to know. Otherwise, let nature take its course, as it surely will eventually.

Male *Litoria infrafrenata* inflating his throat while calling. Photo byLeigh Johnson.

Amplexus

Males call to attract females, and will usually call from or near the water. Willing females should be immensely attracted by this, and will move closer to the males. When a female is sufficiently enthused, she will allow a male to clasp her from behind in an embrace called amplexus. But don't be fooled! Often a male will clasp another male by mistake. If this happens, after a while the clasped male will object and get away. A female is more likely to stay put, although she may decide to leap into the water, carrying the male on her back. This can go on for many hours, sometimes days, the male holding on in the hope that the female will release her eggs in the water. This can get downright dangerous for the female, as she can drown, exhausted from the constant weight of the male on her back, so make sure that there are rocks or plants in the water, so that she can rest when needed.

If this performance goes on over several days, it may be necessary to help the female keep her strength up by feeding her a few insects from tweezers or forceps. Males will usually hold on, even if the entwined pair is lifted from the tank. It's better not to do this of course, as the frogs may well decide not to bother at all, and the female may just retain the eggs until another time. Always make sure that there are rocks or a sloping edge to the water section to give the female an easy exit from the water to prevent a tragedy.

Litoria peronii in amplexus. Photo by Darren Green.

Spawning

When the female is ready, she will release her eggs, which are then fertilised externally by the male. The egg mass will then absorb water and become gelatinous. Sometimes females will wander about and release some of the eggs in inappropriate places; on the substrate, on land plants, all over the place, and there's not a lot you can do about that. Remove these eggs when you're ready, but don't disturb the spawning frogs to do it; it can wait till later. Just be glad that at least some ended up where they were supposed to be, either in gelatinous clumps in the water, or threaded around water plants, as some frogs prefer to do. The female will climb out of the water when she has finished releasing all her eggs. The male may remain in the water though and start calling again for another female. If possible, when the spawning is finished, remove both parents from the tank, or they may well wallow around and break up the spawn into a confusing mess.

Frogs' eggs are usually round and become whitish, with a black stripe also visible. The eggs sometimes, apparently inexplicably, become covered in white fungus. Such eggs are usually infertile and there's nothing can be done. It's a nuisance, but they tend not to affect fertile eggs, so just leave them be until the tiny tadpoles hatch and are big enough to remove to a larger tank where they can have lots more water and room to grow.

If, despite numerous promising starts, and assuming you have both sexes, your frogs fail to breed, then firstly check that temperature, light and water are as they should be. Then consider the frogs' natural habitat. Adjust temperature and humidity to what the frogs would have if in their home environment. Have you adjusted heat and light to simulate the hours of day and night? If not, do this, and allow the frogs to have a cooling period prior to their natural breeding season; this may require temporarily adjusting the lighting to create shorter days for a while. If this doesn't do the trick, then frogs can often be induced to spawn by being sprayed gently with clean water. Only do this when you can hear plenty of calls from the males, usually at night.

After spawning and removing the parents to another suitable enclosure, wait for the tadpoles to hatch from the eggs. This may take a few days or some weeks, depending on the species. Cold climate tadpoles will take longer than those from tropical areas. I don't attempt to remove unhatched spawn from the water any more, as I am not good at wrestling with clingy, slippery spawn. However, if you feel happier removing the spawn, there's no reason not to do so. Use something like a large cup or a dessert bowl, and dip the spawn out very carefully, then lower it gently into the pre-conditioned water in the next tank.

Litoria infrafrenata spawn. Photo by Leigh Johnson.

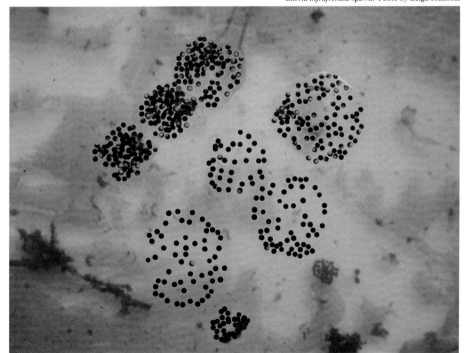

Raising Tadpoles

When the tadpoles hatch, they will be very tiny, and will cling vertically to the glass for several days before they start to swim and feed. When they are all free swimming around the tank, you can remove them to their growing tank. You'll need a fine mesh net to do this, or a small container with which to scoop the babies up, and you **must** have the new tank ready, containing conditioned water, at the same temperature as the water in which the tadpoles hatched. This is a slow job, and must be undertaken with great care if you are not to kill the tiny tadpoles in the process. You'll miss a few, but they can eventually be caught in the net even some days after the initial foray. There will be some algae in the tank water, and this will keep them fed until you can shift them.

So now it's time to grow the taddies on until they morph into little frogs. They need food, clean water and lots of both.

There are many foods suitable for taddies, including some proprietary fish foods, but the best starter food we've used is endive, a leafy green vegetable usually available at supermarkets. Wash it in clean water, and freeze it in small bags. It's a simple matter then to crumble some up and drop it into the water. You can use lettuce instead, but always wash and freeze it; it's not as nutritious as endive though. The taddies swarm all over the food, and they grow like weeds. Tadpoles have teeth, and mouths designed for grazing on algae and other water plants where they find lots of nutrients. You'll have to work out as you go just how much to feed them, and this will depend on the number of taddies that you have, and whether they are indoors our outdoors.

The left over food will make the water murky after a while, so you'll need to make plenty of water changes. Don't try to change all the water at one time; about a quarter can be changed though at any time. Put the fresh water in gently so as not to upset the taddies, as they really hate being disturbed and joggled about. Make sure that the fresh water is around the same temperature as the tank water. As they grow larger, you could add other food, such as small amounts of goldfish or tropical

Photo by Rudie Kuiter

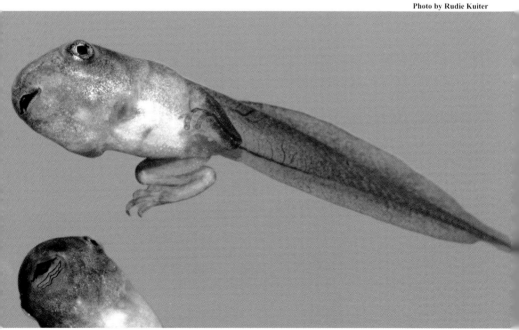

fish food, and perhaps sliced zucchini, or proprietary turtle pellets. Keep an eye on the condition of the water though, and change some frequently to keep the taddies growing. Tadpoles eat their own droppings, so don't get fanatical about cleaning the bottom of the tadpole tank; just replace some of the water on a regular basis.

Tadpoles need lots and lots of water. The more water, the healthier and faster your taddies will grow. Overcrowding will produce small morphlings that are difficult to feed, and frequently die. Some breeders recommend a litre of water per tadpole, but few of us can aspire to this without masses of tanks all over the house. Just give them as much space and water as you can manage.

Metamorphosis (Morphing)

After a time, depending on food, water, number of tadpoles, temperature and species, back legs will appear, so you can see that you're getting somewhere. Later, the front legs emerge, but this will take much longer. Once the front legs have appeared, it's time to move the little chaps again, as if you leave them in the water, and they're unable to get out, they will drown, because they now breathe through their lungs instead of the gills they used as tadpoles. Some floating plants or even floating plastic plants will give them somewhere to rest, and will help prevent drowning until you can remove them to another tank.

At this stage they will still have their tails, and absorb the food stored in there before they need feeding again. It's best to remove them from the water and house them in a frog tank, as you would for adults, with dry land, a shallow water area, and easy access from one to the other. While absorbing their tails, the little frogs like to hide peacefully in moist places, so provide plants, pieces of bark, and cleaned rocks for hiding places.

They won't need feeding until the tail has been absorbed, and then you can start giving them insects suitable to their size. They may look tiny, but frogs will eat anything that they think will fit in their mouths, so keep the food up to them and start adding a little calcium and vitamin powder right from the start, so that their bones grow strong. Keep variety of food in mind, and prepare to be eaten out of house and home.

The little frogs need moist places where they can hide, so make sure to provide properly cleaned rocks, pieces of bark, plants and lots of cover.

If the breeding process has gone according to plan, you may well find yourself with far too many frogs to keep. So, what to do with the excess? They can often be sold to properly licensed pet shops, you could advertise them in a local paper and sell to people with the correct licence, or if you are in touch with a local herpetological society, for reptile and amphibian enthusiasts, you may find a market there.

In desperation, it may be necessary to euthanase some. The safest and most humane way to do this is by freezing them in a container, before deep burial or putting in the bin. This is not pleasant, and shouldn't be routinely undertaken; it's a last resort. Obviously it's best not to breed them if you can't be sure of a ready market.

The one thing you **must not do** is to release them into the wild. Firstly, it is illegal to do so. Secondly, your frogs may be unable to find food, and so starve to death. Thirdly, these little frogs may displace local frogs by eating all of the available food and upsetting the ecology of the area by introducing a non-local species. Fourthly, your frogs may be carrying a disease that you are simply not aware of, and this could be transmitted to an existing frog population, wiping it out completely. Lastly, releasing captive bred frogs unbalances the gene pool in a given area, because you will have raised far more frogs from one set of parents than would have survived to morphlings in the wild.

Litoria infrafrenata metamorphs. Photo by Leigh Johnson.

HEALTH

The most critical issue in maintaining the health of frogs is proper hygiene. Clean air, clean water, a clean tank and furnishings are the surest way to keep frogs healthy. Of course you need to obtain frogs from a reliable, unfailingly clean shop or from a breeder whose facilities meet with careful examination. Look for unfailingly clean premises, clean tanks and water, prosperous looking frogs, and a person who always washes his or her hands or wears gloves before handling frogs. Doing this in the first instance will ensure that your frog keeping is a joyous activity. The next most important issue is temperature. Keep the frogs at the recommended temperature and humidity for the particular species, and more than 90% of potential problems will not occur.

Remember always that a frog's skin allows absorption, and anything in the air, water or general environment can and will be absorbed, so be aware of the potential harm of any products that you may use anywhere around the house, and think clean all the time. If for some reason it is necessary to handle frogs, have on hand a fine fish net made of soft fabric, and move the frogs with that. If this is not possible, then wash, rinse and dry your hands, then wet them again with clean water before you pick a frog up. An option is to only handle them while wearing dampened surgical gloves, which are disposed of after use. Don't handle is the best option; frogs are for watching, not cuddling!

DISEASE

There are probably more diseases that can affect frogs than most of us have ever imagined, and there are also diseases that we can name, and yet know little about. Much, much more work is needed in this area before we can be as sure of a frog ailment as we are with the things that affect cats and dogs. Hopefully every year will produce more information, as many scientists the world over attempt to unravel the mysteries of the decline of our planet's frogs. But even of the diseases and ailments that we do know, there isn't a lot that a novice can do when frogs fall ill. The best prevention is always scrupulous cleanliness, and the quarantining of new frogs before adding them to an existing colony.

If a frog appears unwell, the first thing to do is to isolate it from the others, in the hope that it doesn't have a disease that might be spread to the others in the tank. At least you may restrict deaths in this way. Sick frogs will usually behave differently from the norm; they may sit out in the open when you would expect them to be perching, or may spend very long periods in the water for no apparent reason. But by the time a frog is noticeably sick, the disease has probably already spread.

Take care to wash and dry thoroughly everything that may have been in contact with a sick frog, including your hands and the catching net, as one thing that we do know is that frog diseases spread rapidly, and the more so in overcrowded or less than scrupulously clean surroundings.

If you should be unfortunate enough to lose all of the frogs in a particular tank, then it's absolutely vital that before you even think about getting more frogs, you strip the affected tank down completely, removing everything including rocks, substrate, plants and water. All of the contents of the tank, and the tank itself must be thoroughly cleaned, rinsed and dried. You can scrub the tank out with cooking salt or dilute household bleach, but then it must be rinsed and rinsed and rinsed with copious amounts of water, and dried thoroughly, preferably in the sun. Items of tank furnishings can be cleaned and dried as detailed in *Substrate & Furnishings*, page 8. There is no way to overemphasise cleanliness in the environment provided for frogs. The cleanliness of course must include plants and substrates. Dispose of any materials that may be harbouring disease. Place in plastic bags and freeze thoroughly to kill any harmful bacteria or fungi before disposal.

Chytrid fungus

This is probably the greatest killer of frogs in captivity. It is not unusual for all of the frogs in a tank to die in a short period of time with this disease. The chytrids, the small fungi that cause the disease, live on the keratin on the mouthparts of the tadpoles, and within a few weeks of morphing, the morphlings sicken and die. This is because as tadpoles, the chytrids only live on the mouthparts, but as frogs, the mouthparts are shed, and the chytrids then spread to the skin of the morphlings, which sicken and die. The disease spreads with frightening speed, and should always be suspected if frogs become obviously unwell. The chytrids can remain in the water or any damp areas of a tank, ready to attach themselves to another frog. Symptoms are varied, but may include lethargy, reddening of the inner thighs and lesions on any parts of the body. The most telling symptom though, is that frogs will, uncharacteristically, sit out in the open on the floor of the tank for long periods. Some frogs can apparently carry the fungus without actually succumbing to it. As yet there is no available cure for chytrid fungus, either in captive or wild frogs, and certain diagnosis is not possible without the aid of specialised equipment. The only way to avoid it is to obtain frogs from a reliable source and to always quarantine new frogs. If you suspect this disease, immediately isolate suspect frogs, and take care to handle them **after** all your other frogs to avoid infecting them all. A vet may be able to send samples off for identification of a specific disease, but that isn't going to help you, as by the time it is diagnosed, the frogs may well be dead.

Overcrowding and stress

Both are potential factors in frogs becoming sick. It's not possible to suggest numbers of frogs to square centimetres of tank, but do give your frogs plenty of room to move about the tank, and always underestimate the numbers of frogs you can keep, rather than overestimating and causing problems. Frogs can become stressed by being moved from one tank to another, being handled, having inappropriate temperature or humidity, incorrect lighting, overcrowding, or having their keeper endlessly fiddling about the tank and disturbing the inhabitants. Get the tank well set up before you add the frogs, then all should be well.

Redleg

This is a bacterial disease and is also fast to spread. Prevent this by scrupulous cleanliness with attention given to basic care. Affected frogs can develop pinkish or reddish colouring to their legs, and this may be all that you see until the frog is obviously sick and ultimately dies. Unfortunately, no available cure exists for this disease either, and the best you can do is to dismantle and clean the tank and furnishings to avoid further outbreaks. Isolate suspect frogs quickly, and hope to contain the disease. However, some frogs normally have pinkish or reddish inner thighs naturally, so if you keep such species, expect to see this colour even on healthy frogs, eg. Blue Mountains Tree Frogs and Green Tree Frogs.

Injuries

These sometimes occur, where a frog cuts itself on something sharp in the tank. Clearly, avoiding all sharp edges is vital. But if you see a frog with an injury on any part of its body, the best advice is to remove the frog to an isolation tank and seek help from an experienced vet. Many of the antiseptics that we commonly use in our homes will be quite unsuitable for frogs, so don't use any creams or lotions, just keep the frog relatively dry until a vet is able to treat it.

Soft bones/metabolic bone disease

This occurs only when frogs are not obtaining sufficient calcium and vitamin D3 in their diets (see *Feeding* and *Lighting*). Calcium deficiency shows up as uncontrolled twitching and spasms of the back legs. Affected frogs will be obvious, as they have trouble moving about the tank. They may be hunched or twisted, but by the time this is noticed, it may well be too late for remedial treatment (it is possible though for vets to administer an injection of calcium under certain circumstances). Prevention in the form of calcium powder right from the start is the key.

COMMON QUESTIONS AND ANSWERS

Q. Why do frogs' eggs often grow fungus and fail to hatch?
A. Eggs that grow fungus are frequently infertile, and probably won't affect the fertile eggs in the rest of the spawn, so just leave them until the others hatch. Avoid breaking the spawn apart. Sometimes eggs may grow fungus due to a fungus in the water. To prevent fungus growing on eggs, you can use an anti fungal additive, a product containing malachite green, in the water. These products are usually manufactured for fish, so carefully read the directions, and if no dosage rate is recommended for frogs, use at half the strength of that recommended for fish. You might just be cunning enough to add the product to clean water before the spawning.

Q. Why do lots of tadpoles seem to die?
A.There are several possibilities here. Check that the water the taddies are in has been properly conditioned and is at the right temperature. If there are lots of taddies, overcrowding and the resulting stress may cause deaths. Allow as near as possible to a litre of water for each tadpole. Give them the biggest container you can find, with lots of surface area for oxygen. To increase oxygen in the water, use a pump and air stone as sold in aquarium shops; just a gentle bubbling will help. Avoid too much disturbance of the water, as the taddies will have to fight against the current. A fact that

might help you feel less guilty, is that in the wild, only about 5% of tadpoles grow to be adult frogs. It's almost inevitable that some tadpoles and small frogs will die. However, large-scale deaths indicate a serious problem, possibly due to overcrowding or perhaps a water quality problem, so check these carefully. If you're doing better than occurs naturally, you're not doing too badly.

Q. Why do tadpoles sometimes seem to have a big bubble of air inside them? When this happens, they can't swim properly.
A. Bubbles of air can form inside taddies if you add fresh water too quickly, or from a height. Try to pour the fresh water gently down the inside of the glass, rather than tipping it all at once. Remove affected taddies and put them into a small container (a cup will do for one tadpole), then only just cover them with water. After a few hours or days, the air bubble may well disappear. No feeding is needed while you wait for the bubble to disappear.

Q. How long is it necessary to quarantine new frogs before releasing them into an established tank with other frogs?
A. A minimum of two months is essential, but six months is better, as some diseases may take that long to show up.

Q. What's the best way to transport eggs, tadpoles and frogs?
A. With eggs or tadpoles, they need to be jostled about as little as possible, so put the spawn or taddies in a container with some of their living water. Fill the container almost to the top with more of the same water, and put a firm lid on top. Small bottles are good for just a few tadpoles, as they allow less movement than a jar. If travelling for more than a short distance, stop and remove the lid for a few minutes to allow air exchange. Remember to allow temperatures to equalise before releasing the spawn or taddies into their new tank. To transport frogs, use a soft plastic container like an ice cream container, and line the bottom with a good layer of damp sphagnum moss to cushion them while travelling. Secure the lid down after ensuring enough air holes. Make the holes from the inside to the outside to avoid the frogs being scratched by sharp edges.

Q. Why do frogs sometimes look as though they're itchy, and wriggle and squirm as if they're having a fit?
A. Frogs, like reptiles, have to shed their skins periodically, and this process certainly looks uncomfortable. They tend to shed from the back of their bodies towards the front, bringing the shed skin over their heads, at which point they usually eat the skin. This definitely looks alarming, but is a regular occurrence. See photo on page 10.

SPECIES

As it's clearly not possible here to give all of the information for every Australian frog species, I have listed only the most commonly kept frogs. If you have frogs that are not listed here, refer to the information for a similar species, and make decisions on whether to heat or not, according to the locality where the frog naturally occurs, and the difference between that and your own area. When selecting the frogs you want to keep, ensure that the particular species is legal for keeping in your state. Note that frogs may be kept outdoors only where the climate matches that shown on the map for that species. Otherwise keep inside with heating as specified. Humidity if required, can usually best be achieved with dense planting in the tank. The plants will need periodic watering, and will grow faster and lush with frequent spraying. If the humidity rises to the stage where condensation is running down the inside of the glass, then the level is probably too high except for those frogs listed as needing high humidity.

GREEN TREE FROG
(Litoria caerulea)

GENUS: *LITORIA*

Frogs of the *Litoria* genus have adhesive discs on their toes. These discs enable them to hold onto surfaces for climbing. Their other distinguishing feature is that the pupils of their eyes are horizontal.

Also known as White's Tree Frog.

Size: Can reach 100mm.

Colour: Most often a bright green, with a 'plastic frog' look. Can change to olive green, and can also have white spots. Under surface is cream /off white.

Call: Deep throated 'crork ... crork..crork' at night.

Heat: Not needed unless the temperature where they are housed drops below 10°C for days at a time. I have kept and bred these indoors in southern Victoria for many years at house temperatures. However, if buying from a source where heat has been used, you may need to keep this up and reduce the heat gradually.

Humidity: Prefers a dry environment when kept indoors.

Breeding: Spawns in summer. In colder areas, it can be beneficial to warm juveniles just a few degrees above ambient temperature, although this is not essential.

General: These are easily the most popular frogs of all. Their big bodies, laid back attitude, and smug expression, along with their ease of maintenance, make them deservedly the most often kept of all Australian frogs. Green Tree Frogs can live for 20 years, perhaps more if conditions are right. They eat everything put in front of them, and will eat far too much for their own good, so watch a tendency to over eating in these already solidly built frogs. Prefers to perch near the top of the tank, and sleeps most of the day. Vertical tank recommended, with wide perching shelves.

Photo by Darren Green.

WHITE-LIPPED FROG
(Litoria infrafrenata)

Also known as the Giant Tree Frog.

Size: To 110mm.

Colour: Usually a bright green, but sometimes dull green or brown above. A distinct white stripe on the lower lip reaching back to above the beginning of front leg. White underneath. A narrower body than the Green Tree Frog, and a much narrower head and face. When calling, males may exhibit pinkish stripes on the legs.

Call: A very loud 'Curraaak, curraaak ... curaaaark' endlessly when really in top gear. Can deaden the sound of conversation or television, and the neighbours will be deafened too.

Heat: Needed unless you live in the area of natural habitat. About 28°C recommended; a little higher in summer.

Humidity: Prefers a humid environment; an aquarium heater in the water and a partially covered top to the tank will do the trick.

Breeding: Spawns at the drop of a hat in summer; encouragement not needed.

General: This is a glorious frog with wonderful colours. The male's calls will possibly drive you insane, but he does stop once spawning has been achieved, and thankfully will be silent until next spawning time. These frogs often wallow about in the water and need sufficient depth to do this; at least 100mm depth preferred. A skittish frog that jumps at shadows, and often grabs at fingers in its enthusiasm for food. I wouldn't be without these giants; my absolute favourite. Can be cannibalistic. Vertical tank recommended, with very wide perching shelves.

Photo by Darren Green.

RED-EYED TREE FROG
(Litoria chloris)

Size: To 65mm.

Colour: Bright to dark green above with white or yellowish underside. Thighs may be reddish to brown to purple. Eyes are distinctive with golden iris, often ringed reddish.

Call: Alternates between gentle trills and long mournful 'aaaark .... aaaark', usually after rain.

Heat: Not usually needed unless the temperature where they are kept falls below 10°C for days at a time. If this is so, a temperature around 18°C to 24°C is adequate most of the year.

Humidity: Likes some humidity; so mist spray in the enclosure every few days in summer.

Breeding: Frequent spraying when males are calling in late spring to summer, will encourage spawning.

General: This is a peaceful little frog with many devotees. Goes quietly about its activities without fuss. Can be somewhat on the fragile side unless everything is absolutely right. But once you've got the enclosure conditions settled, it will live happily and spawn regularly. Vertical tank recommended.

Photo by Mike Swan.

BLUE MOUNTAINS TREE FROG
(Litoria citropa)

Also known as the Variegated River Tree Frog.

Size: To 65mm.

Colour: Light brownish dorsal area, often flecked darker, and with a dark brown stripe from nose through eye and along body. Brown dorsal areas and under the eyes can be edged with green. Groin and insides of thighs are bright orange/red. White underneath. An occasional frog can lack the brown and be all green.

Call: 'Creek….bobble, bobble, bobble.'

Heat: Not necessary. In fact you <u>must</u> keep these frogs cool, even turn the lights off in really hot weather.

Humidity: Low; spray occasionally in hot or very dry weather, and to encourage spawning.

Breeding: Spring and summer. Usually spawns readily, given a large enclosure.

General: This is a beautiful and easy to keep frog in cooler areas. Likes to perch high under the light. Often found lurking under rocks or tucked into plants. Likes a well planted tank and about 100mm. of water depth to spawn. Include lots of rocks to simulate its natural home. Keep water very clean, and preferably moving by way of an air-stone. These frogs wouldn't dream of cannibalising their young. Loves to leap and jump. Vertical or horizontal tank with tall planting. Provide wide perching places.

Photo by Mike Swan.

PERON'S TREE FROG
(Litoria peronii)

Size: To 50mm.

Colour: A most distinctive frog, which is dark brown to grey to cream above, but changes colour often. May have green flecks and some dark mottling. Groin, armpits and backs of thighs are black/ brown with bright yellow marbling. Underside is white or cream. This is the only Victorian frog with cross-shaped pupils.

Call: A really maniacal cackling in a descending scale; sure to terrify visitors who haven't heard it before. 'Ah…ah…ah…ah…ah.' Calls loudly and persistently through spring and early summer.

Heat: Not needed unless temperatures fall below 10°C for days at a time. In this case, use an aquarium heater to maintain around 15°C water temperature.

Humidity: Likes plenty of humidity in summer; spray lightly every few days in summer.

Breeding: May breed mid spring to mid summer, but can be reluctant in captivity. Encourage with frequent spraying when males are calling. Can be challenging to breed.

General: A spectacularly beautiful and different frog. Likes plenty of climbing area during the day, but goes hunting on the ground. Plants should be taller growing types to allow these frogs to indulge their climbing ability. Vertical or horizontal tank with tall perching places.

Photo by Darren Green.

DAINTY TREE FROG
(Litoria gracilienta)

Also known as the Banana Box Frog.

Size: up to 45mm

Colour: Variable, from bright green to pale green above, with pale yellow or cream underneath. Thin yellow stripe runs from the nose through and past the eye.

Call: A prolonged 'weeee' or sometimes 'waaaaa.'

Heat: Required south of Sydney in winter. Around 25°C winter temperature is sufficient, but may be increased by several degrees in summer.

Humidity: Likes to be kept on the moist side in a well- planted tank. Fond of climbing, so branches or tall plants should be supplied.

Breeding: Usually breeds readily in summer after rain. Mist spray to encourage spawning.

General: A very pretty little frog, which is often found well out of its northern range when it is accidentally transported south in boxes of bananas. Vertical tank recommended.

Photo by Mike Swan.

GREEN AND GOLDEN BELL FROG
(Litoria aurea)

Also known as Green and Golden Swamp Frog.

Size: Grows to 85mm and is a big bodied frog.

Colour: Variations of green, usually with blotches of gold or bronze. A whitish stripe and a thinner dark stripe run from above the nostril through the eye and down along the flank. White underneath. Groin area is blue to blue-green. Occasionally individual frogs may be all gold or all green.

Call: A throaty and loud 'craw-ark, craw-ark, crok crok' , often a three part call.

Heat: Not usually needed, as this is a frog from cool areas.

Humidity: Likes a moist environment, and is an aquatic frog, living always close to ponds and dams.

Breeding: Through summer, but can be earlier. Mist spraying when males are calling will encourage spawning. Keep the water area really deep (120mm at least), for the frog to swim, wallow and dive.

General: This frog is a greedy feeder, often active during the day. Has been known to cannibalise. Keep frogs of this species together only when all are of a similar size or the small ones will be eaten. Active during the day, and likes to bask under the lights. A beautifully coloured, shining frog. For whatever reason, this species is not currently thriving in the wild. Keeping and breeding this beautiful and distinctive frog can be challenging. Vertical or horizontal tank, with tall perching places due to high UV light requirements.

Photo by Greg Fyfe.

DWARF TREE FROG
(Litoria fallax)

Size: To 25mm.

Colour: Can be green or fawn above, but sometimes flecked darker. White stripe runs from below eye level to just under the front legs, and the groin area is orange/yellow.

Call: A continuous 'Reek-pip, reek-pip' from water's edge or from nearby vegetation at night.

Heat: Not needed unless kept far south of its home range, or where temperatures fall below 10ºC for days at a time. In this case use an aquarium heater to maintain around 15ºC. We have kept these indoors in Melbourne very successfully without heat.

Humidity: Prefers a little moisture during the breeding season, but always provide dry areas, and tall plants for the frogs to rest during the day.

Breeding: Late spring through summer, usually after rain.

General: The Dwarf Tree Frog is thoroughly charming, and a constant source of delight in the house. Easy to keep and breed, and an enthusiastic feeder. Strong frogs despite their tiny size. The fastest at escaping! It seems to be out even before you lift the lid. Vertical or horizontal tank will suit. Supply high perching places.

Photo by Mike Swan.

SOUTHERN BROWN TREE FROG
(Litoria ewingii)

Size: To 45mm.

Colour: Creamy brown to dark brown, often with dark flecks. A dark brown/black stripe from the nose through the eye and continuing to the shoulder. Underneath is creamy to white. Several different strains of this frog will have colour variations; some almost solid green, and a very appealing one with broad green and brown stripes the length of the body.

Call: A melodious 'weep, weep.'

Heat: Not needed. Can be kept outside even in the far south, as long as you obtain locally bred specimens. Not a frog to try in the north unless cooling can be provided.

Humidity: Moderately moist environment preferred.

Breeding: Usually late winter. Strings its spawn like fairy lights around water plants.

General: The Browns are the easiest of all easy care frogs. Happy in the simplest enclosure as long as they have material to climb and perch up near the top of the tank. Melodious mass calling at night. These are very hungry little frogs. Vertical tank recommended.

Photo by Darren Green.

GROWLING GRASS FROG

(Litoria raniformis)

Also known as the Warty Swamp Frog.

Size: To 85mm.

Colour: Bright green with gold, bronze and sometimes brown/black irregular spots. Groin area including backs of thighs can be turquoise. White underneath with warty looking skin on the back.

Call: A growling 'waaah, waaah' often likened to a motor cycle changing gear. Males call while floating in the water.

Heat: Not needed, as this is a frog of the far south. Not recommended for keepers in warm districts unless cooling can be supplied.

Humidity: Happy in a moist environment and active after rain.

Breeding: Spring, sometimes summer. Frequent mist spraying will encourage spawning.

General: Will do well in outdoor enclosures with plenty of water area and low growing cover. Active

Photo by Darren Green.

GREAT BARRED FROGS
(Mixophyes balbus/fasciolatus/fleayi/iteratus)

Size: 80 to 115mm.

Colour: Yellowish black through soft brown to nearly black above. Their most distinguishing feature is that all have conspicuous banding on their legs. Thin blackish stripe through the eyes almost to the shoulder. White underneath, and toes are about three quarters webbed.

Call: Varies within the group from deep grunts, a sad chorus of 'Aaaaaaah', to single 'Op, op, op', or 'Cook, ook, ook, craaak.'

Heat: Not needed if frogs are obtained from local breeding. However, if keeping *M.fleayi* in the far south, some extra warmth is indicated; around 18°C water temperature is suggested from our experience. There is one other in the genus, *M. schevilli*, from the far north, which will certainly require more heat.

Humidity: All these frogs are from damp habitats, so the tank should be kept moist without becoming soggy. (Use the tap under the land area often to prevent souring of the substrate). Always allow some large, smooth flattish rocks or pieces of bark, and plenty of soft substrate for burrowing, which is what these frogs do during the day. Leaf litter can be provided.

Breeding: Late spring to early summer. Males call from the banks of creeks, and that is where the eggs are laid, only being washed down into the water in the next rain. So make sure that you can provide a slope where this is possible, and you can create the 'rain' with a hand sprayer or gentle spray from a hose. Prefer to spawn near running water which, with a little ingenuity, can be created with a pump connected to a small air-stone with gentle bubbling.

General: There are five frogs in this species, all big frogs, and all from damp areas on the eastern coast, and for the general purpose of keeping, all are treated similarly here. These are glorious frogs with incredibly beautiful eyes, but not the frog for the complete beginner. Definitely a challenge to keep, and especially to breed. Best to save these until you gain lots of experience with easy to keep species.

Photo by Darren Green.

STRIPED MARSH FROG
(Limnodynastes peronii)

Size: Up to 65mm.

Colour: Greyish brown or light brown above, with darker stripes. There is a white stripe from below the eye to near the armpit, and occasionally a white stripe runs down the back. White underneath. Almost no webbing on the feet.

Call: 'Plok' or 'Whuk' very loudly. Males call while floating in or very close to the water.

Heat: Not needed, as long as specimens are locally bred.

Humidity: Likes moist places such as swamps and dam surrounds, so ensure plenty of cover on the land area, in the form of dead leaves, bark, low growing plants etc.

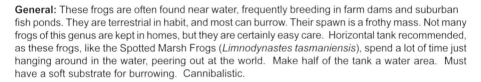

Breeding: An enthusiastic breeder in spring and summer. Tadpoles grow very large, and may take over a year to morph.

General: These frogs are often found near water, frequently breeding in farm dams and suburban fish ponds. They are terrestrial in habit, and most can burrow. Their spawn is a frothy mass. Not many frogs of this genus are kept in homes, but they are certainly easy care. Horizontal tank recommended, as these frogs, like the Spotted Marsh Frogs (*Limnodynastes tasmaniensis*), spend a lot of time just hanging around in the water, peering out at the world. Make half of the tank a water area. Must have a soft substrate for burrowing. Cannibalistic.

Photo by Darren Green.

SPOTTED MARSH FROG
(*Limnodynastes tasmaniensis*)

Also known as the Spotted Grass Frog.

Size: Up to 45mm.

Colour: Light brown to olive green on the back and legs, with irregular darker blotches. Often a pale orange or yellowish stripe runs from the nose down the back. A pale stripe runs from below the eye and almost reaches the armpit. Belly is white and smooth. Very slight webbing on the feet.

Call: Repeated and very fast 'uk uk uk', sometimes 'pok pok'. Kept indoors, this call in the breeding season is every bit as maddening as an ancient Chinese water torture.

Heat: Not needed, assuming you obtain locally bred specimens, as this frog naturally ranges from eastern Queensland down through Tasmania.

Humidity: Likes to hide in damp places, so keep some parts of the land area damp, and some dry. Provide low hiding places.

Breeding: Spring to autumn. Tadpoles grow very large, and may not morph until the following year.

General: A happy little frog that loves to hang about in water, with just his nose and eyes sticking out, so make sure that the water area is quite large, perhaps half the tank size. Provide low cover in the form of bark or river stones and low, thick vegetation. Branches are not needed, as Spotties spend most of their time on the floor of the enclosure. Horizontal tank recommended. Can cannibalise, and can climb rather too well for a frog without adhesive toe discs.

Photo by Darren Green.

PAINTED BURROWING FROG
(Neobatrachus sudelli)

Size: Up to 40mm.

Colour: Considerable variation possible, from greyish through yellowish/olive brown to red brown above, with spots and blotches on a warty looking skin. Creamy stripe down the centre back is likely. Underneath is creamy white and smooth. Toes have full webbing.

Call: Short trills repeated as the males float in the water.

Heat: Not needed, assuming locally bred specimens.

Humidity: As they are usually in burrows, keep the deep and soft substrate moist but not sodden, and include low growing plants. Very fine gravel or fine sand, rather than palm peat is what we have found suitable for the top layer of substrate, with plenty of low growing plants, pieces of bark and some small rocks for cover.

Breeding: Late summer after rain is usual. Eggs are laid in strings around water plants.

General: Intriguing, fat little frogs, which spend all day hidden in their burrows, only emerging at night to feed. Horizontal tank recommended, with about a third to a half being water section. These really are charming little frogs that seem to sit upright, showing their pale throats and bellies. Their call is always a delight.

Photo by Darren Green.

SOME VITAL REMINDERS

DO'S
1. Do use a tank with drain holes and taps in both land and water areas.
2. Do always start with a completely clean tank.
3. Do boil or bake any rocks or pieces of wood that you use as frog furnishings.
4. Do ensure that the water you use is suitable for frogs.
5. Do obtain a light suitable for reptiles and amphibians.
6. Do feed your frogs on live food.
7. Do use a calcium/vitamin supplement.
8. Do quarantine all new frogs for a minimum of two months.
9. Do flush your tank through regularly on both sections with clean water.
10. Do provide dry areas in the tank.
11. Do provide climbing material for tree frogs.
12. Do vary the diet for your frogs.
13. Do use frequent part changes of water for tadpoles.
14. Do provide easy access to, and exit from the water for all frogs.

DONT'S
1. Don't crowd frogs or tadpoles.
2. Don't handle your frogs unless absolutely essential.
3. Don't use any kind of sprays, eg. deodorant, air freshener, fly spray etc. in the house.
4. Don't paint near the frogs with high gloss paint; the fumes are deadly.
5. Don't smoke or use incense in the house.
6. Don't use water from the hot tap.
7. Don't keep different species of frogs in the one tank.
8. Don't keep small frogs in the same tank as bigger ones; the small ones will probably be eaten.

ACKNOWLEDGEMENTS

This book is for Mousie who truly understands the magic of the frogs.

The book could not have been written without the experience of all those who have kept frogs before me, and whose knowledge was so generously shared when I first started on the great frog adventure. My grateful thanks also to the frogs who have given me the pleasure of their company over so many years.

REFERENCES

Bartlett, R.D. and Patricia, P. (1996) *Frogs, Toads and Treefrogs*, Barrons Education Services, New York.

Cogger, H.G. (2000) *Reptiles and Amphibians of Australia,* Reed New Holland, Australia.

Hero, J.M., et al. (1991) *Frogwatch Field Guide to Victorian Frogs*, Dept. of Conservation and Environment, Australia.

Robinson, M. (1998) *A Field Guide to Frogs of Australia* (From Port Augusta to Fraser Island Including Tasmania), Reed New Holland, Australia.